HATS

AND THE COWBOYS

WHO WEAR THEM

HATS

AND THE COWBOYS

WHO WEAR THEM

TEXAS BIX BENDER

GIBBS SMITH
TO ENRICH AND INSPIRE HUMANKIND
Salt Lake City | Charleston | Santa Fe | Santa Barbara

Revised Edition
21 20 19 18 17 16   20 19 18 17 16 15 14 13 12 11 10 9 8 7 6 5 4

Published by
Gibbs Smith
P.O. Box 667
Layton, Utah 84041

1.800.835.4993 orders
www.gibbs-smith.com

Cover Design by Black Eye Design
Book Interiors design by Kurt Wahlner
Printed and bound in the U.S.A.

Gibbs Smith books are printed on either recycled, 100% post-
consumer waste, FSC-certified papers or on paper produced
from a 100% certified sustainable forest/controlled wood source.

The Library of Congress has cataloged the earlier edition
as follows:

Bender, Texas Bix. 1949–
Hats and the cowboys who wear them / Texas Bix Bender.
p. cm.
ISBN I3: 978-1-58685-191-0 (first edition)
ISBN 10: l-S8685-191-8 (first edition)
I. Cowboys — West (U.S.) — Costume — Humor. 2. Hats —
West (U.S.) — Humor. I. Title.
F596.B333 1994
391'.43 – dc20

ISBN 13: 978-1-4236-0702-1
ISBN 13: 1-4236-0702-3

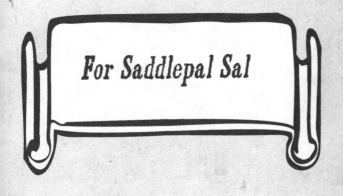

For Saddlepal Sal

A tip of the hat to National Cowgirl Hall of Fame master hatter Sheila Kirkpatrick, Sean Attendito of the Stetson Hat Company, and, of course, to John B. Stetson, the man who started it all.

DISCLAIMER

THE OPINIONS expressed in this book are at best half-assed, and the author does not intend to back them up in any alley.

CONTENTS

A Cowboy's
History of the Hat

Hats have always been worn for one of two reasons: either to impress somebody with who you are, or to help you in your work. The first hats seem to have been worn by tribal chiefs to let everybody know they were the boss. Then the spirit guides got into the act to let everybody know they were in touch with the Big Boss in the Sky.

But when men and women began to work with the land, they needed something to protect their heads from the elements. It didn't matter what the hat looked like or who it impressed—which was probably nobody. What mattered was how it worked. And people probably started to have competitions to create the best hats: the biggest, most artistic, best use of natural resources—the usual kind of contests. And maybe people became more impressed with the hat as a status symbol than as useful clothing.

As time went by and people got fed up with high-hatting, non-working nincompoops, things did a 180, and the only hats that folks continued to wear were ones that worked. And of all the hats that work, the one that works best is the cowboy hat:

- It gives your face and neck shade from the sun.

- It keeps your head dry when it rains, sleets, snows, or hails.

- You can use it to fan a campfire to life, whip a fighting cow away, or swat a bucking bronc on the neck.

- You can use it for a pillow.

- You can use the crown to carry water for your horse and the brim as a cup to water yourself.

- It protects you from low-lying branches.

- You can use it to signal somebody far away.

- Tossing it in the air tells the world you're happy.

- Not only does it work for you, you look good in it.

COWBOY HATS

No one knows for sure, but cowboy scientists working at MIT (Montana Institute of Technology), as well as many other hat historians, believe it all started with the Mongol hordes. This is not as bizarre as it sounds. The Mongols rode small maneuverable horses; they were expert riders and could do anything on horseback they could do on foot. They thrived on the bare necessities, had little use for luxuries or liars, and – until the cowboy – were the greatest horsemen who ever lived. So, like the cowboy, the Mongol needed good boots, a good saddle, and a dang good hat. (Of course, cowboys had better manners and except for Saturday nights, did not tend to make war on the civilian population.)

When the warring Mongols tried to invade

10

Europe, they didn't make it. But their hats' wide brims did, and when the Spaniards caught on to it, they adapted it into a flat-topped sombrero and brought it to Mexico with them.

Over the next three centuries, the Mexicans developed vast cattle ranches, and the vaqueros who tended the herds modified the hats into the *sombrero* and *poblano*. (*Sombrero* comes from the Spanish word *sombra*, which means "shade.")

The first Americans to come into Texas combined the slouch hat of the Southern Planter with the sombrero and came up with a floppy-brimmed, high-crowned cowboy hat. For the next fifty years, American cowboys wore versions of all these hats and then some.

Then in the late 1860s, a Philadelphia hatter named John Batterson Stetson came west seeking a cure for his tuberculosis. Camped on the side of Pike's Peak after enjoying several weeks of the delightful extremes of western weather, he decided his small-brimmed, small-crowned Philadelphia hat was pitifully inappropriate. So he took a hatchet, a pocketknife, and some other camping tools and made a fine felt out of rabbit and beaver

11

fur. Next, he fashioned the felt into a high-crowned, wide-brimmed hat.

It was a big hat, one that could shelter a man from rain, sleet, hail, and snow; from sun, wind, dust, and low-lying branches. A hat that suited the big country, the West. Shortly after he made it, a passing cowboy sitting in a handsome saddle astride a high-spirited stallion saw Stetson in the hat and offered him five dollars for it. It goes without saying that five dollars was a nice piece of change back then. Stetson was more than glad to sell him the hat. No record exists to tell us exactly what this hat looked like, but when John B. Stetson returned to Philadelphia in 1870, he couldn't get the image of that cowboy wearing the hat out of his mind. He made some more of them, named them "The Boss of the Plains," and sent them out as samples to dealers all over the West. The orders poured back. The Texas Rangers wanted one for every man with a badge. Within a decade the name John B. Stetson became synonymous with the word *hat* in every corner and culture west of the Mississippi. Custer was wearing a Stetson at the Battle of the Little Big Horn.

When Stetson died in 1906, his factory was turning out 4 million cowboy hats a year!

★ ★ ★

HAT RULES OF THUMB

The higher the crown and the bigger the roll on a man's hat, the more cattle he runs. Of course, it could also mean he's been getting a lot of rain lately: a big roll funnels water off. Of course, it goes without saying, the more rain you have, the more grass, and the more grass, the more cattle, and therefore the bigger the hat.

Cattleman

Whether it's a pint-sized spread or a ten-gallon size, if you own and run it, and if there's any kind of cattle on it, you're a cattleman. But a lot of ranches are owned by somebody in the city and run by somebody else. This has given rise to the saying, "A cowboy has a big buckle over his belly; a cattleman has a big belly over his buckle." But, whatever, you don't have to be a cattle baron to wear a Cattleman's hat. You just have to have a hankerin' to be one.

A lot of bankers and politicians are partial to this hat. It has that cattle-rich successful look to it. There's some sentiment going around that this hat attracts sassy, classy city cowgirls to a feller's corral.

The buckaroo who wears it probably likes to sing and yodel when he's driving his pickup or when he's in the shower. He might even sing under a lady's balcony. And why not? After all, George Strait wears one and look what it's done for him.

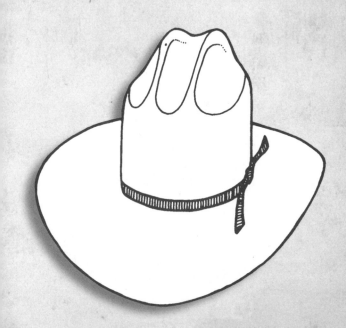

BULL RIDER

The buckaroo or buckarette who wears this hat really knows how to throw the bull . . . pitch the bull . . . roll with the bull . . . and, especially, shoot the bull.

BRONC RIDER

The wearer of this hat likes to open the chutes and let 'er rip. If there's a nag to be ridden, a fiddle to be danced to, or a kiss to be stolen, this hombre will be the first in line. He won't give out either. He don't quit 'til the horse is gentled, the dance is over, and the kiss grows cold.

No, this buckaroo is not a TV repairman or an electronics salesman. RCA stands for Rodeo Cowboys Association, and this is the hat style they opted for many moons ago. It was also a very popular style with the movie cowboys of the 1940s and 1950s.

The fella who favors this style is looking for a ride that bucks like a bobcat with its tail afire. And once this jasper gets in the saddle, he won't get off unless he's thrown forked end up. But when the ride's over and the bucking stops, he's off, without a backward glance, looking for another ride.

Years later, though, sitting by himself around the campfire, he remembers every ride.

MONTANA
Pinch

This is also known as the Smokey the Bear. Highway patrolmen and military drill instructors favor this hat. The cowboy who wears it tends to take things kinda serious. He likes to be the boss but don't care much for being the bossee. He probably has a pretty rigid set of rules he likes to live and judge by. In spite of all this, every now and then he likes to wear woolly chaps (pronounced "shaps") and howl at the moon.

MONTANA SLOPE
(OR MONTANA PEAK)

(Also known nowadays as the Gus Slope, after the Robert Duvall character in *Lonesome Dove*.)

A deep crease down the front of the crown is a practical matter when you're working where it rains a lot. The crease acts like a trough and funnels water off the crown. A man who wears a hat like this when it ain't raining ain't worried about rain.

Matter of fact, ain't much does worry him. Oh, he might keep a wary eye on the horizon to see what's ahead, or shoot a glance over his shoulder every now and then to see what's coming, but

that don't mean he's worried. Just cautious.
Like when he buys a new standup-collared
shirt, he saves the receipt just in case things
don't work out. He's a man who knows where
to find the handle to get a grip on things.

Southwest Peak

You'll notice this looks a lot like the Montana Pinch—yet it don't. The crown is higher, the brim is wider, and the pinches are longer and more sloping. This fella is a real range rider. His hat is one of the oldest styles in the West. He's not much for cities. His home is truly on the range. His pickup may not be the latest model; in fact, it may be beat all to hell—but it's likely in tip-top running shape. His horse is probably not very flashy either, but it knows how to work cattle and go all day without coming up lame. He talks to the things he loves: the land, his horse, his pickup, his cattle—he even talks to his wife if he has one.

Open Crown

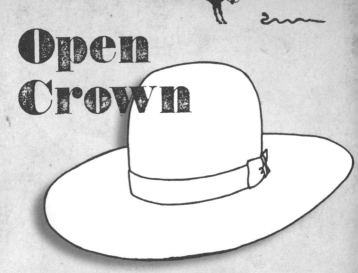

here are no creases anywhere on this hat. Could be this hombre thinks he looks good enough that his hat don't matter. On the other hand, he might just like to keep things simple. Or on the third hand, it might be that he's never bothered to give his, or his hat's, looks any thought whatsoever. Whichever one it is, he'll tend to be pretty spare in his thinking. He won't give a lot of thought to frills, creature comforts, or comfortable creatures.

23

MULEKICK

ou get a mulekick crease by taking your fist and punching it into the crown of your hat. The indentation that's left looks kinda like a mule's hoof.

The cowboy who wears a mulekick in his hat don't like to do a lot of explaining. He don't want to hear any whining. He just

24

wants to get the job done and he's durn sure he knows how to do it.

If he's got one mulekick on the side of his hat, he's probably getting a little set in his ways.

If he's got one on both sides . . . well, he's pretty much figured out the way he likes things done.

If they're on both sides and in the back, he'll stand toe-to-toe with you over just about anything.

And, oh my, if he's got them on all four sides, he got them directly from the Great Spirit Himself. Okay, if it's a woman, The Great Spirit Herself.

No matter what
you wear,

if you wear a cowboy
hat on your head,
you'll be called
a cowboy.

TWO DOT

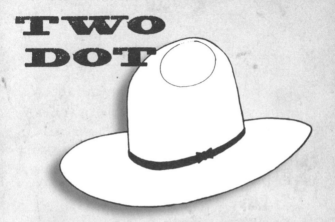

The Two Dot probably comes from the High Plains, where everything boils down to two choices: get ready for winter or get ready to cross that Great Divide. The jasper who wears a Two Dot seems to like things in pairs. He sees two of a kind as a good balance. He'll be hard to corner 'cause he'll always have two ways in and two ways out. He'll have two pairs of boots and two hats. Two trucks, but only two cassette tapes—George Jones and Willie Nelson. He'll probably just have one wife, but he'll also pay a lot of attention to his dog.

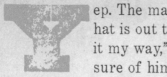

THE FOREMAN

ep. The man who wears this hat is out to run the show. "Do it my way," he explains. He's sure of himself and tries real hard to do it the right way – the way that won't need redoing anytime soon. He might be stubborn and a little quick-tempered, but it's because he's purty durn sure he's right and anybody that disagrees with him ain't. He'll not be picky about his own creature comforts, but by dang, you'd better not mistreat his critters or anything else that looks to him for care. Lite beer will be an abomination in his eyes, as will salads as the main course. He wants meat and potatoes; forget the wine and the whining. But a little whiskey in the evening is just fine. If you eliminate the small talk, he can carry on a pretty decent conversation.

★ ★ ★
HISTORY OF THE BLOCKHEAD

IF YOU WENT to a hatter in the sixteenth century, he'd measure your noggin and then carve a block of wood to match its exact shape and dimensions. This chunk of wood was called a blockhead. The hatter would then make you a hat and block it to your blockhead.

Sometimes people would become confused whether they were talking to you or your blockhead and . . . well, you can imagine the rest.

TEN GALLON

This hat is so big, it tends to make you think big. So, buckarettes, if you've got a guy who's thinkin' small, give him this hat as a present and see if it don't make him stand taller and give him ten-gallon ideas – even though it's only holding three quarts. The Ten Gallon hat came on the scene around 1925. It's highly unlikely any working cowboy ever owned one. The immense sky pieces were popularized by Tom Mix and other Hollywood buckaroos. Drugstore cowboys liked them. So did photographers, 'cause anyone who ever saw a Ten Gallon hat wanted their picture taken wearing it.

CUTTER

This wrangler has a good eye for what he wants and is very adept at getting it. He can spot a maverick and separate it from the herd slicker than melting butter on a hot knife. He's got similar moves when it comes to two-stepping a filly around the dance floor. His problem comes when it's time for words, not actions. He'd a whole lot rather just keep quiet and keep moving.

TOM MIX

Tom wasn't the first to wear a hat with two off-center Montana slopes, but he was the first to wear a really big one. So, most folks nowadays call this hybrid headgear the Tom Mix hat. The fella who wears one is apt to be a true lover of the romance of the West. He loves to sing "Tumbling Tumbleweeds," has a set of real longhorns hanging in his den (maybe even on the hood of his Dodge Minivan), thinks a great vacation would be two weeks on a real working ranch, has everything the Sons of the Pioneers ever recorded, and calls his wife "buckarette." And when they watched *Lonesome Dove* together, he was the one who cried when Gus died. He's all right.

HIGH PLAINS

This one is also known as North Country or Up North. John Wayne wore one kind of like this, but his had a mulekick in the back. It's a big hat and the man who wears it usually has big ideas. He probably rides a big horse, has a hill-size, extra-cab pickup and lives in a big house – or at least a double-wide. He likes his hot dogs foot-long, his beers in tall-boys, and his women with big hair. His favorite team is the Denver Broncos; his favorite singer is Dolly Parton; and his favorite actor is . . . you guessed it.

10 COMMANDMENTS OF THE COWBOY

1. Do not take unfair advantage of an enemy.
2. Never go back on your word.
3. Always tell the truth.
4. Be gentle with children, elderly people, and animals.
5. Do not possess racially or religiously intolerant ideas.
6. Help people in distress.
7. Be a good worker.
8. Respect women, parents, and the nation's laws.
9. Neither drink nor smoke.
10. Be a patriot.

AUTRY CREASE

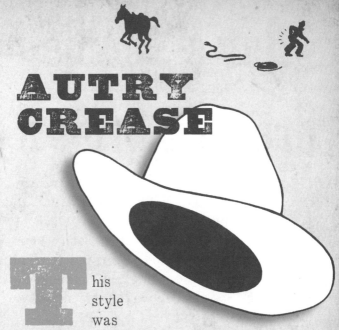

This style was popularized by America's Favorite Cowboy. It has a single crease down the middle and one on each side of the crown. This is a no-nonsense hat. Gene Autry was a no-nonsense singing cowboy from Oklahoma. In the public eye he represented (and still does) his "Ten Commandments of the Cowboy."

The fella who wears this hat today is more than likely a working cowboy—or an insurance salesman who, as a kid, got Gene Autry six-shooters every birthday.

Roy's Double-Creased Crown

Roy Rogers was a real flamboyant cowboy. Not since Tom Mix in the Roaring Twenties had anybody seen such flashy attire. Roy could ride, rope, shoot, and yodel in great style, and he did it in great clothes too, including his Stetson. He wanted his skypiece to be unique, so he put modified RCA creases on both sides of the front of the crown, then added his own invention—the double telescope crease on the top. (Dale Evans wore a regular flat-topped telescope with stampede strings. It's her hat that's pictured here.)

These days, Roy's Doubled-Creased Crown is not seen too much outside of cowboy discos. The dude who wears one likes the glamour and romance of the West but doesn't really want to live it. He probably owns a luxury sedan, wears boots that have never sniffed manure, and spends more time on his Blackberry than in the saddle.

It takes from two to six **HOURS** to **MAKE** a hat.

BUTTERFLY

This hat is worn by a snappy dresser who acts and looks successful. He probably is doing fairly well, but not nearly as well as he likes to act. His pickup truck will be loaded with options. He'll especially love to show you how the power seats go all the way back. His saddle will have enough silver to send a metal detector to the promised land. He takes himself and his belongings very seriously. He makes his payments on time, and he'll probably retire to that condo in Scottsdale some day.

Goat Roper

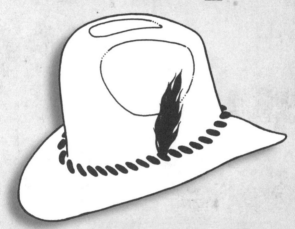

This dude likes to throw 'em and tie 'em. He just don't wanta get dirty doing it. Four-legged critters confuse him a bit, though not any more than two-legged ones. But he's nothing if not willing. He probably rides a moped, or a walking horse, and has a lot of fun doing it. If he has his druthers, he'd druther not get wild 'n' woolly.

POPPER

The "brush popper" was the cowboy who went after the cattle in the mesquite thickets of Texas. It was not an easy job and you had to be a pretty tough hombre to do it. When you're chasing cattle through a mesquite jungle, you have to go pretty fast while the brush whips and pokes and pulls at your skin and clothing with a dedicated fierceness.

Anything loose gets ripped away. So a brush popper kept his outfit to the bare minimum. Nothing fancy, nothing extra, nothing that could snag and get torn off. He even used a shorter rope and a smaller loop than a regular cowboy.

This conservatism carried over to his hat. He kept it pretty lean and spare, no creases on the sides, and with just a small indentation on the top of the crown.

The man who wears the Popper today probably has a little of that old-time brush popper in him. He likes things lean and mean. He finds the most efficient way to do anything. He's neat and not too tolerant of a mess. For something to make sense to him, it has to work. For a woman to make sense to him, she has to be logical. But even if things fall apart and don't work out, he won't give up. He'll just try to fix it so it works better next time.

Centerfire

The first saddles in the West were Spanish rigged; that is, they had a single cinch that was directly under the forks, just below the horn. The early Californians thought this was a little rough on the horse's belly; it tended to chafe. So they moved the cinch to the middle of the saddle and called it a center-fire rig.

This hat started out in California too, and since it had a single ridge running down the center of the top of the crown, it was called a centerfire.

The man who wears this hat is apt to be wearing a tie or a neatly knotted silk scarf. His trousers sport a sharp crease, and you won't find him in jeans very often. He likes the idea of the gentleman rancher, sort of the Ronald Reagan type. This fella can actually walk through a barn without getting a speck of manure on his boots. He likes classic cars, fine whiskeys, and women who like to hear him talk. But then, what man doesn't?

"Little Miss Sure Shot"
Annie Oakley,

Buffalo BILL,

CALAMITY JANE,

and

Wild Bill Hickok

all wore

STETSONS.

Rimrock

imrock is the steep rock that runs along the rims of the canyons all over the West. It's nearly impossible to climb and very dangerous to be around. Wherever you find it, the bottom is a long ways off. A man or a horse that treads the rimrock had best be clear of head and sure of foot. One slip and you can kiss your Angora woollies goodbye.

The man who wears his hat with two steep rimrock creases tends to be sure of himself, sure of what he's doing, and sure of where he's going. His only problem is he keeps his head down to check each step and has a hard time seeing anything that's not right there. This is only a problem when he's not riding the rimrock.

45

HAND

Hand," in this case, don't refer to what you put in your pockets when you're nervous, but instead what you do for a living. It's short for cowhand. A cowhand is a cow puncher, a cowpoke, a cowboy. They all mean the same nowadays, but they didn't used to. Originally a cowpoke or a cowpuncher was the fella who prodded cows onto cattle cars to be hauled to market. To call a cowhand a poke or a puncher was sort of degrading. But to be called a "hand," or especially a "top hand," has always been considered complimentary. The words all came to mean the same when Hollywood

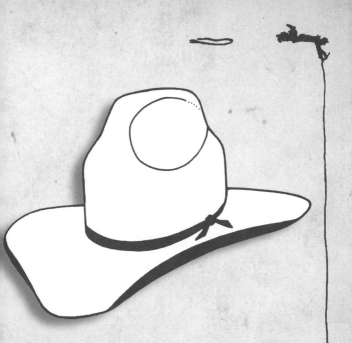

discovered the cowboy and his quaint
language.

The man who wears the Hand
nowadays probably is a hands-on kind
of feller. He won't call and tell you
how to do something. He'll come over
and show you how to do it. But when
he lends a hand, he expects you to
watch and learn, 'cause he don't plan
to show you twice.

They say:

the higher
the crown, the
more cattle.

Of course,
high crowns
have also led to
the saying

"All hat and
no cattle."

BIG PEAK

This hat became popular in the 1940s. It's sort of a cowboy fedora. The man who wears one today more than likely sees things as big or small. And a lot is always better than a little. His pizza will be loaded like his six guns, he won't care much for small dogs, and won't even bother to notice cats. Steaks will start at one inch thick, and if they're under a pound he'll toss 'em back. He'll favor an automobile over a pickup, and it will be a Buick or bigger. Foreign cars are too small, too ugly, and too . . . foreign. He will want his wife to have big hair and big appetites. 'Course, that don't mean she'll have any of these, but he'll love her in spite of it.

Horseshoe

The galoot that sports this beaver lid tends to think the world is his Rocky Mountain oyster. He'll have a smooth answer to any question. You'll seldom find him feeling down. Anything wrong today can be fixed tomorrow. A deck of cards, a pair of dice, or a horse race holds great promise for the future. He'll have a pickup truck weighted down with chrome, a wardrobe of tailored polyester clothes, and a horseshoe diamond ring to match his hat crease. He'll happily promise a woman the moon and it'll be hers to look at ever after. 'Course, on the other hand, it could just be that he likes horses and wants to wear a hat that reminds him of them.

⚞ Sidekick ⚟

I t takes an ornery feller to wear a hat that looks this bad. He just don't care what you or anyone else thinks. Matter of fact, he don't think much of thinkin'. He don't think he needs to bathe, he don't think he needs to change his underwear, and he don't think he needs to change his ways one iota. He don't have a lot of friends, but he don't think he needs 'em anyways. Of course, if he's a sidekick, there must be someone who'll put up with him. Pity them.

★ COWSTEP ★

his hat gets its name 'cause it kinda looks like a cow stepped on it. It's the little peak in the front of the crown that a wearer is looking for, though. The cowstep look to the crease is just an accident of that.

The galoot who puts this skypiece on his noggin tends to like to get things moving, then stand on a knoll and look heroic. He's a good organizer and doesn't hesitate to take charge and run the show. Now, that don't mean he's gonna get down in the wagon ruts and get his manly hands covered in grime, or wash dishes, or do laundry or anything like that. That would not look heroic.

Telescope

This was the favorite cowboy hat of the 1950s. Every western TV star wore one of these. Matt Dillon wore a white one, Bret Maverick wore a black one, Cheyenne wore one, Steve McQueen wore one, even Annie Oakley wore one. But not too many real cowboys wore one, other than the drugstore variety.

The type of dude who wears one nowadays was probably a kid in the fifties. On the job he likely doesn't wear a hat of any kind, unless it's a hard hat. He rents western videos, loves to watch late-night reruns of *Gunsmoke*, and wishes everyone everywhere lived by the Code of the West. So do I.

HAT  BANDS

Hatbands come in all shapes, sizes, and styles. The basic function of one is to tighten the crown of your hat to fit your head, but not many folks wear one for that reason these days. Nowadays the hatband is there just for looks. You can pick yours from an endless variety of styles, from braided horsehair or silver conchos to Indian beaded, kangaroo leather, or a simple piece of ribbon. Your choice, your hat, your head. Whichever one you choose, though, will tell a lot about who you are.

Hat Feathers

The kind of cowboy who wears a feather in his hat probably rides a Peterbilt with more horsepower than a herd of the wildest ponies. He drives cattle not by the hoof but by the ton, along with anything else that needs to be moved. He's torn between Richard Petty being the king and Elvis, who is the king.

Of course, there's also the turquoise hat with lots of feathers that you win at the state fair and only wear until you sober up.

The

Marlboro man

wears a

Resistol

hat with a

Cattleman's

crease.

Australian Bush Hat

he only reason cowboys "down under" wear this floppy wonder is because nobody named John B. Stetson ever emigrated down there. The bloke who wears this hat tends to have a reckless outlook on life. It's a wild 'n' woolly work hat, not meant to be a fashion statement, though that don't stop a lot of folks from wearing it anyway. The wearer favors jeeps over pickups, knives over guns, and prefers a cold beer to chardonnay any day, mate.

TYCOON

This hombre is top hand when it comes to puttin' on the dog. He leaves a cloud of dust wherever he goes. He don't ever walk on tippy-toes. The sun is supposed to rise when he crows, not the other way around. He carries a roll as big as a wagon hub or he don't go out. He likes to use words that run eight to the pound and can talk a doorknob into believing it's a dinner bell. He's a lot of fun to be around.

FOUR CORNERS

This is a very even hat, and the man who wears it is probably a very even-handed, squared-away person. He'll be neater all the time than most men are on their way to church. His shirts will be crisp and freshly ironed. His pickup will get frequent washings and regular waxings. There won't be any empty beer cans in the bed of it neither, but if he ever does leave one lying around it'll be neatly crushed and pressed. He's no doubt a good two-stepper, and he spends a good deal of time admiring his shadow.

You'll see hats with braid worked around the rim and it's mostly done for style nowadays. But the practice started when a poor cowboy could only afford a cheap, floppy hat. To keep the brim from flopping, he'd make slits all around the brim and weave leather braid around it and then tie it in back. This stiffened the brim and helped hold its shape.

DUDE

The dude that favors this hat is a fancy dresser. If he has cattle dealings of any kind he uses a computer and a telephone. He likes his Lone Star served in a pilsner glass. At dinner he likes his waiter to have a French accent and his beef to be bloody rare. (A real cowboy likes his steak burnt.) When it comes to romance he don't need to use a lot of kindling to get a fire started. He's okay for a dude; just be sure to cut the deck a little deeper than normal when you're dealing with him.

★★★★★★★★ PACKER

The ramrodder who wears this skypiece believes in getting the freight delivered. He'll have a big pickup and won't mind if you call him up and ask him to give you a hand moving a piano. He might want to cut it into smaller pieces so it'll fit in his truck better, but he'll get the dang thing moved. He likes to line dance, but you'd better stay in line and look sharp or he'll give you a helpin' hand and then some.

Stampede Strings

The hombre who wears these hat holders likes to go to hell for leather and wants his hat to go with him. He won't spend a lot of time thinkin' things over, and waitin' for things to develop will not be his style. He'll wear out a lot of saddles 'fore he picks a home corral.

EL PRESIDENTE

Stetson's top topper, 100X, pure beaver. This skypiece comes in its own glass showcase with a certificate of authenticity signed by the president of the Stetson Hat Company. The felt is so fine and perfect that it's not much thicker than a manila envelope. You hardly know you're wearing it. However, you will notice a flatness in your wallet if you pop for one: the El Presidente goes for around $1,500. It comes only in white, and while it gets dirty real easy, its quality felt cleans up very nicely.

The only thing you can say about the man who wears this hat is that he's fifteen hundred dollars lighter, but he's got a real good-looking hat.

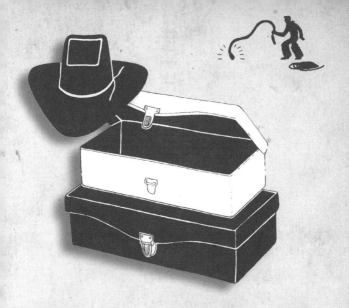

BOX SLOPE

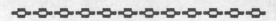

 ou gotta work at liking a hat like this. The feller who wears one takes a little gettin' used to too. He'll probably like to box everything up like his hat crease. He'll like pizza 'cause it comes in a box, Volvos 'cause they look like a box, and, of course, he wears boxer shorts.

FLAT-TOP BRIM

A flat-topped hat with a flat brim takes itself very seriously, and so does the joker who wears it. He measures his words and weighs yours very carefully. Best not to joke around this fella; his idea of fun probably ain't yours. In other words, he won't get it and you might. He tends to be a loner and generally misunderstood—this is mainly 'cause he don't bother to explain himself very much. He won't dance 'cause he don't like crowds.

The woman who wears this hat won't like to be crowded either, but that don't mean she won't dance.

The more beaver in a hat, the lighter it is.

EVEN PEAKS

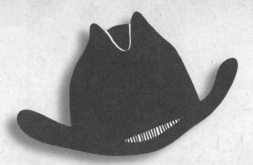

This is a really well-balanced hat. The brim comes up in a precise curve on either side. The two peaks on the top of the crown are perfectly apportioned, and the whole hat has a positive flow. No wonder cowboy accountants prefer this skypiece three to one. It has a businesslike look, even comes in a gray pinstripe, and it gives their domes pretty good protection when I.R.S. agents start beatin' 'em over the head with new tax laws every year. And since they've pulled out most of their hair or lost it due to worrying over other people's money, they need hats to keep their heads warm.

The
OLDER
a hat is,

the
lighter
it is.

HIDE HAT

This hat is made entirely of cowhide and is, well, tough as leather. It's also hot as hell. It's virtually indestructible. A horse can trample it, a mule can kick it, a cow can "let go" over it. It might show a scar or two, but it'll hold together without a give. This makes it the perfect headgear for the kind of man who drives a jeep. He can run around with the top off, and when the wind blows his hat off, he can go back and get it and it'll be none the worse for wear—even if the eighteen wheeler coming along behind him has run over it. Plus, it looks real dashing on him when he takes his jeep off the road and goes careening around the countryside, tossin' out one empty beer can after another and generally raisin' hell while tearing up good grazin' land and ruining as much of nature's fragile beauty as possible.

To make a cutout, the hatter cuts the design out of the crown of the hat and then glues or stitches a piece of dyed leather on the inside of the hat to cover up the hole. (Sounds like a lot of extra work to me.) Sometimes he or she will also weave a piece of leather around the outside of the brim that matches one of the cutouts. All this is done strictly for looks, and the fella who wears one of these unique toppers is obviously looking to stand out in a crowd. He figures if folks notice his hat, they'll notice him. If the hat doesn't work by itself, he's likely to start singing or playing a musical instrument. If this fails to get their attention, he'll start telling jokes or doing old Stan Freberg routines or even tossin' out quotes from books like *Don't Squat With Your Spurs On!* If after all this he still is being ignored, he'll throw himself on the floor and roll around imitatin' varmint dances. Not a pretty or polite thing to see. I recommend you notice his hat to start with and avoid all the rest of his disgustin' display.

CUTOUT

Mountain Man

The man who wears this hat is not expectin' it to help him meet women, get a loan at the bank, or be invited to join the Chamber of Commerce. All he wants his hat to do is keep his head dry if it's rainin', warm if it's cold, and shaded if it's hot. That's good, 'cause that's about all this hat will do. This topper ain't fancy and neither is the man who wears it. He likes the simple life. He don't like a lot of company and he don't say much, and it ain't safe to load him up with questions. He likes to rough it—and if you don't, he ain't much fun.

RANCHER

The jasper who wears this hat may or may not be doing well, but he sure looks like he is.

He's the kinda man that either has a big bankroll of hundred-dollar bills, or has a big bankroll with a hundred-dollar bill on the top and the bottom and a hundred one-dollar bills in between. He either owns a late-model Cadillac or owes for one. His luck might run muddy, but his hopes never run dry. He's a snappy dresser and fun to be around 'cause he's always the first to reach for the tab—even if he's gonna write a bad check for it.

✂ Gambler ✂

I f fate tempts the dude who wears this skypiece, he'll take the bet and double down. Chances are he'll lose, but that won't stop him from playing again. Every turn of the cards is a new game. Tomorrow is right now, and a rainy day is not worth saving for. He might be fun, but when the chips fall where they may and it ain't his way, he walks away.

Straightback

If you'll notice, this hat has a straight, uncreased flow from front to back. The only affectation is a very neat hatband and two very deep, very precise creases on either side of the crown. This is one uncluttered hat. The feller who wears it probably likes everything neat and clean like his hat. He combs his hair straight back, knocks his shots straight back, and sits in straight-back chairs. I wouldn't use the phrase "anal retentive" here, because I don't know what it means, but I'll bet this hombre counts how many sheets of toilet paper

he tears off at a time. (It's important to reiterate that I will not step into any alley to defend anything I say here.)

WESTERN DERBY

Bat Masterson wore one of these. So did a lot of other gamblers, piano players, bob-wire salesmen, and other non-cowboy types. I own one myself. It belonged to my wife's great-great-granddaddy, who was a circuit preacher in Texas. He only wore it on Sundays, and I generally only wear it on Sam Houston's birthday (March 2) or New Year's Eve.

The fella – other than me, of course – who wears a derby nowadays, is probably something of a dandy. He gets his hair cut every week, wears lightly starched shirts, can tie his own tie, and the boots he wears when he wears his derby are never scuffed or scarred. He'll usually have a deal or two goin' on that he'd like to interest you in, and if you've got the money, he's got the time. He'll be more apt to put a diamond on his pinky than a woman's finger. And he's probably never been closer to a cow than a T-bone steak.

Horse Soldier

Not much reason for anybody to wear this hat anymore. 'Course, there's no reason why anybody who wants to can't, either. The roughrider who wears one of these toppers probably likes to make statements like, "It's exactly forty miles to Mission Wells," rather than, "Oh, I'd say it's about forty miles or so." Instead of asking you if you like something, he'll ask, "Your steak is good?"

Now, if you're a woman married to this hat wearer and gettin' ready to go out to

dinner, do yourself a favor and don't
ask him how he thinks you look –
unless you really want to know.

This fella's dog will know a lot
more than just how to get in the
pickup when it's told. By the way, his
pickup will be beat all to hell from
goin' where it didn't wanta go but he
insisted it did. And he'll have a purty
good idea of what's fair and what
ain't . . course, it'll be *his* idea.

There is no
standard X rating.
It's up to the hatter
how many X's he
wants to rate a hat.
This makes it real
important to know
your hatter.

Hat Lingo

HAT IN HAND – This one's as plain as a new saloon in a church district. Your hat is worn on your head, the seat of who you are. It is your most prideful adornment. You only take it off to show respect or if you feel humble before someone, and not many hombres who wear a cowboy hat feel all that humble. It's always been this way.

Cowboy's Working Hat

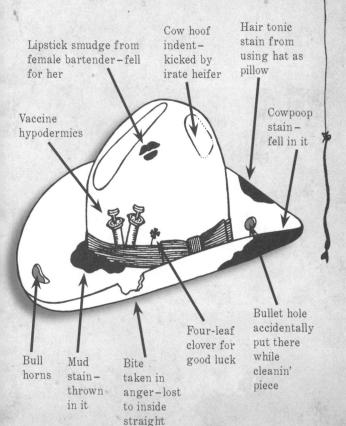

Lipstick smudge from female bartender—fell for her

Cow hoof indent—kicked by irate heifer

Hair tonic stain from using hat as pillow

Vaccine hypodermics

Cowpoop stain—fell in it

Bull horns

Mud stain—thrown in it

Bite taken in anger—lost to inside straight

Four-leaf clover for good luck

Bullet hole accidentally put there while cleanin' piece

Appendices

for

SERIOUS

or

Not-So-Serious

HAT

FOLKS

TIPS FOR WOMEN

It is my opinion that you should wear what you like. But here's what the fashion experts say:

- Petite women should wear small-brimmed, small-crowned hats.
- If you want to look taller, go for a little higher crown with a slope crease.
- Tall women should wear wider-brimmed, shorter-crowned hats. Try a telescope or RCA crease.
- Full-figured women should avoid high crowns and go with curled brims and dramatic creases.
- If you have a long face, put a big curl in your brim and keep away from narrow shapes.
- If you have a round face, go with a higher crown, but stay away from round brims.
- If you have an oval face, you've got the perfect face for any hat you want to wear.
- If you have a triangular face, go with a small brim with a big roll and a high crown.
- If you have a square face, try a peaked crown and a curled brim, and wear your hat at an angle.
- Whatever way you go, never wear your hat on the back of your head, tilt it, pull it down, or wear it straight.

THE TEN HAT
COMMANDMENTS

1. Never handle your hat or anyone else's by the crown. It leaves fingerprints and breaks down the fabric. Always pick up a hat by the brim, and adjust it on your head by holding the front and back of the brim.

2. The safest place to keep your hat is on your head.

3. Anytime you take it off, set it upside down on its crown. Otherwise it'll lose its shape and all your luck will spill out, too.

4. Never leave your hat in a hot car, closet, or anywhere else that gets hot. It'll shrink.

5. If you get caught in the rain and your hat gets wet, let it dry out slowly. Same reason as above.

6. Never put on anybody else's hat, and don't take it kindly if they put on yours.

7. If you're handing somebody their hat, give it to 'em upside down, back towards you. Otherwise, if they don't look, they're apt to put their hat on backwards. This is bad luck and you'd look bad too.

8. When you meet a woman, tip your hat to her.

9. Take your hat off if you sit down at a table to eat. Leave it on if you're at a counter.

10. Once a week wipe your hat with a sponge, and when it starts to get loaded with trail dust, have it blocked and cleaned by a professional.

PICKING
YOUR HAT

Before you even try a hat on, give it a thump with your index finger. A good hat should have a nice thump to it. It should be buoyant and bounce back nicely.

Check the number of X's stamped on the sweatband. The more X's, the more beaver, the more beaver, the better the hat. A hat with less than four X's probably isn't a very good hat. If it has twenty or more, you'd better be prepared to spend upwards of four hundred dollars.

While you're looking at the sweatband, make sure its genuine leather that's been sewn in, not glued. A plastic sweatband is a

waste of time, and any sweatband that's not sewn in won't stick around for long.

Try the hat on. If it's the right size, it should come down to just above your ears. If it's too big, but the next size down is too small, the secret is toilet paper. Fold some up and stick it inside the sweatband. Cowboys have been doing this since they started wearing hats. It helps the fit and you're ready for unexpected emergencies on the range as well.

As for which style is right for you, you want the height of the crown and the width of the brim to be in proportion to the shape of your face and the width of your shoulders. The old rule of measure is that the height of the crown should be equal to the distance from your chin to the middle of your forehead. The wider the brim, the wider your shoulders should be.

One last tip, no matter what style hat you wear, the flat, uncurled part of the front brim should be as wide as your face.

why the hatband bow is on the left

It goes back to the knights of the Middle Ages. When a man went into battle, he wore his lady's feather on the left side of his topper to show his love for her. He stuck it in the left side because he was generally right-handed, and putting it on the left side kept it out of his swordplay. Of course, if he was left-handed, he had the choice of being a slave to fashion or being cut to ribbons when his sword got entangled with his lady's feather.

HAT-ISMS

TALKING THROUGH YOUR HAT – This one's been pegged to a specific time, a specific place, and a specific person: New York, May 13, 1888, an interview in *The World* entitled "How About White Shirts?" It seems there was an effort underway to get New York streetcar conductors to wear white shirts like their counterparts in Chicago. When the reporter asked a New York conductor what he thought of these efforts, he was quoted as replying, "Dey're talkin' tru deir hats." No one needed this explained to 'em.

HAT ON THE BED – Most folks believe this is bad luck. It is if you lay down on your hat and squash it. Seems the expression comes from way back when people believed in evil spirits – other than the ones you drink. These evil spirits lived in the hair. This probably came from static electricity in the air crackling and

91

popping when you came in and took off your hat. So, the idea was, don't lay your hat where you're gonna lay your head 'cause evil spirits are spilling outta the hat. It doesn't make any sense. But then, superstitions seldom do.

EATING YOUR HAT – There ain't no such thing as a sure thing. But that's where this expression comes from. If you tell somebody you'll eat your hat if they can do something, don't be wearin' your best hat, just in case. The expression goes back at least as far as the reign of Charles II of Great Britain and had something to do with the amorous proclivities of ol' Charlie. Seems they named a goat after him that had his same love of life, which included, in the goat's case, eating hats.

OLD HAT – Old, dull stuff is old hat. This one seems to come from the fact that hat fashions are constantly changing. But hat fashions haven't been changing for all that long, so the expression seems to have gotten its start around the turn of the century.

MAD AS A HATTER – This one is as old as felt hats. It means utterly, totally, completely demented. The Mad Hatter in *Alice In Wonderland* was a personification of this expression. In fact, the original belief that led to the saying couldn't have been more wrong.

Early hatters used mercury in the making of their felt. Their bodies absorbed mercury, and after several years of making hats, the hatters developed violent and uncontrollable muscle twitchings. The ignorance of the times caused people to attribute these strange gyrations to madness, not mercury. Nowadays, they don't use mercury and the expression makes even less sense than it used to. Although, I know some hatters who can go right off their mental reservation and act like popcorn on a hot skillet if you get too far behind on your bill.

TIGHT AS DICK'S HATBAND – You don't

hear this one much anymore. The Dick in this case is Richard Cromwell, the son of England's seventeenth-century dictator Oliver Cromwell. Richard succeeded his dad and wanted to be king but was quickly disposed. The hatband in the phrase refers to the crown he never got to wear.

Why a **COWBOY** Wears His Hat the Way He Does

his official guide was developed after some intensive research in a number of waterholes from Nacogdoches to Nashville and with a lot of help from cowgirl Lisa Miles and her amigas.

If a cowboy is wearing his hat pushed back on his head, that's a good sign if you're a single cowgirl, 'cause it means he's single too – and lookin'.

On the other hand, if a jasper's wearin' his Stetson pulled down low so the brim is shielding his eyes, look out. He's on the prod too – but he's married!

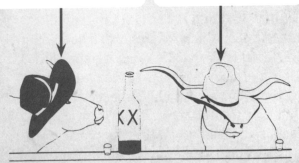

NOWADAYS a lot of cowboys are wearin' this style of hat to keep from bein' mistook for truck drivers.